How to Draw
101 Really Cute

Characters

TOP THAT™

Licensed exclusively to Top That Publishing Ltd
Tide Mill Way, Woodbridge, Suffolk, IP12 1AP, UK
www.topthatpublishing.com

D1357620

Princess Cutie Pie

Love Bunny

Moo Moo Cow

Little Bow Wow

Unifaun

Pretty Kitty

Koal-ahh

Bubbles

Flick the Fairy

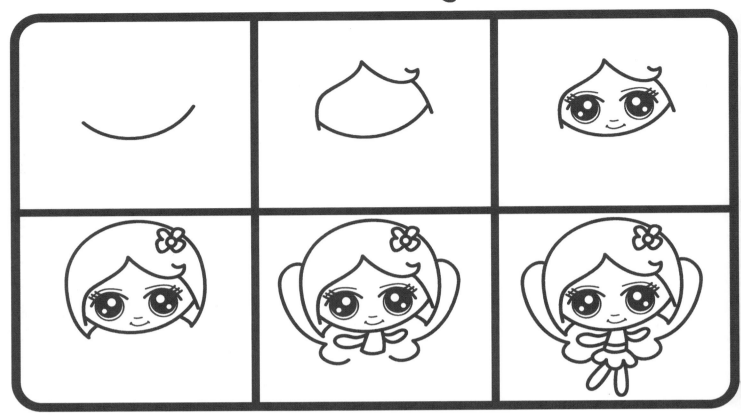

Chirpy

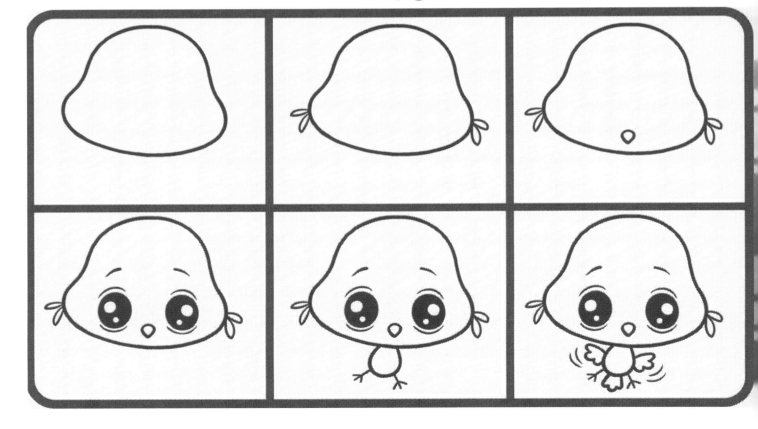

Munchkin

Bear Hug

Poodle Pooch

Fluffy

Puggle

Flame

Loxie

Dizzle

Trunky

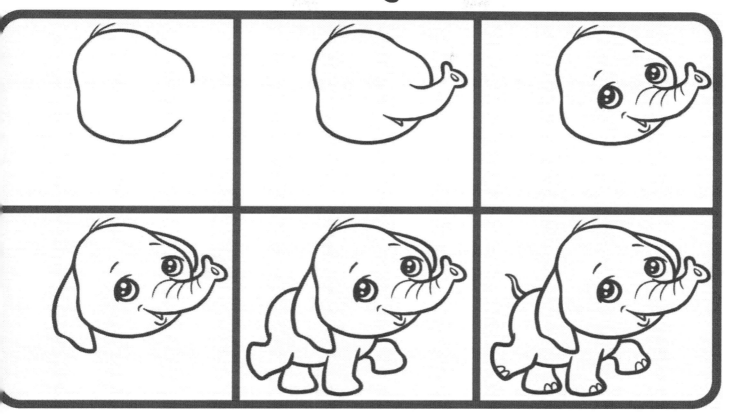

Ickle Lion

Puppy Love

Piggle

Sweetheart

Nibbles

Giggles

Pawpaw

Tiny

Pinkee

Sneezachoo

Tumtum

Snugglekins

Clopsy

Belle

Bluebell

Wiggly

Snowdrop

Waddles

Oinki

Tinky

Pandaisy

Splash

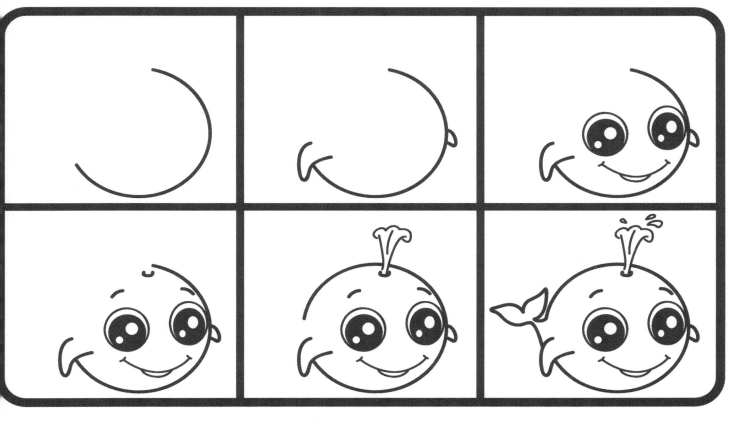

Tiddles

Bichon

Angel

Tangle

Groovy

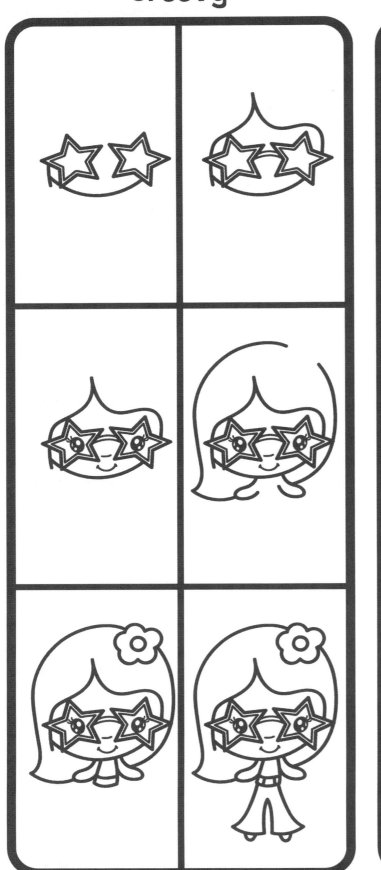

Yodel

Bluey

Foxy

Tinchy

Kimmi

Oo-la-la

Curly

Izzy

Baby Pengiun

Dreamy

Daisy

Tizzle

Tickle

Wobble

Waffles

Snuffles

Lolly

Whirligig

Buzz

Divine

Poppy

Nectar

Huggles

Sweetie

Melody

Loople

Pootle

Noobles

Harmony

Peekaboo

Froggle

Tiggy

Cherish

Starbright

Moonbeam

Cherub

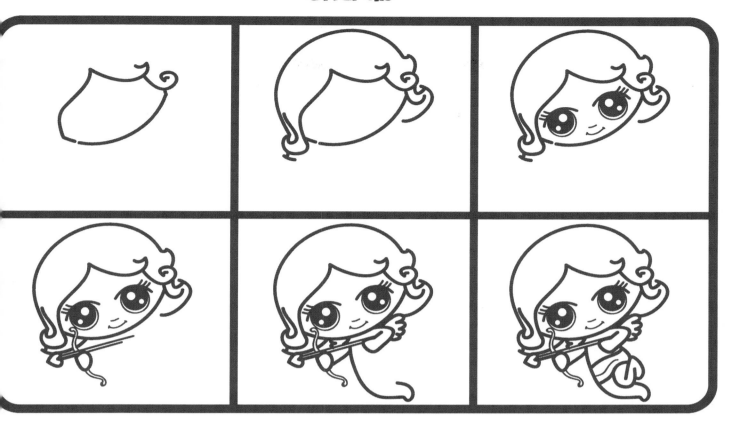

Wriggler

Smiler

Rainbow

Milly

Doggy Woggy

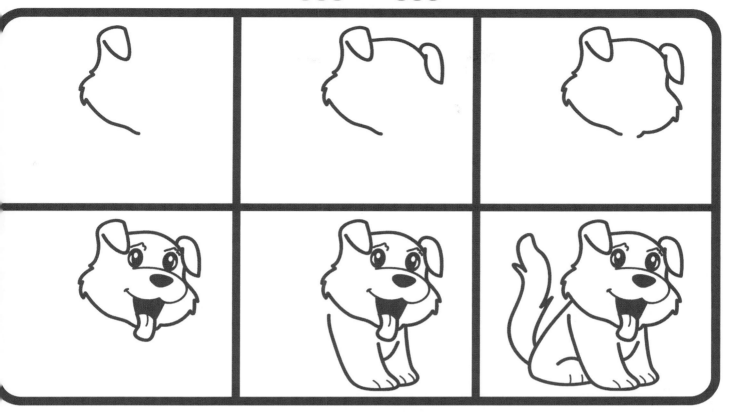

Sunshine

Boo Boo

Wifflebug

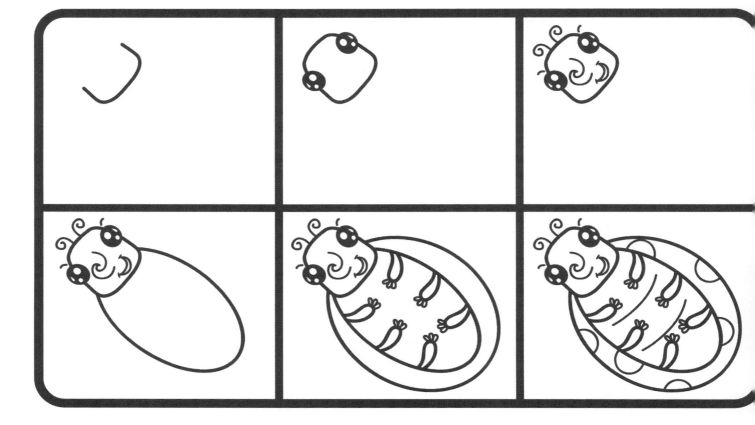

Happy

Scaredy Cat

Delicious

Pickle

Kissy Kissy

Faun

Dopple

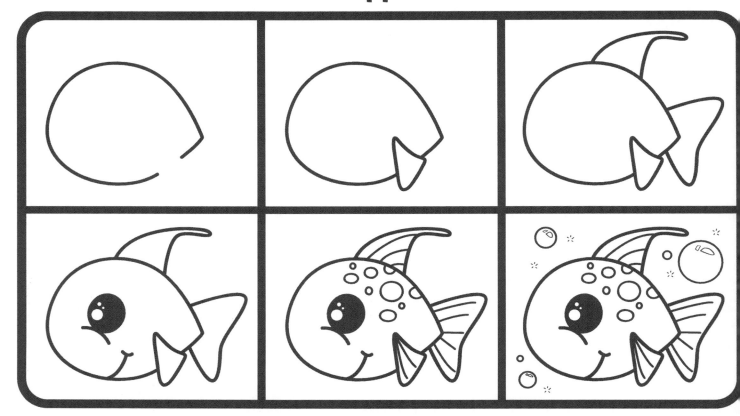

Topsy

Blink

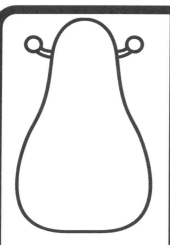 

Cotton

Cuddles

Other titles in the 'How to draw' series:

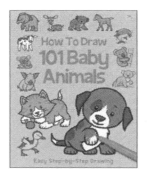
978-1-84956-987-3

978-1-84956-608-7

978-1-78244-484-8

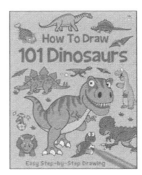
978-1-78244-021-5

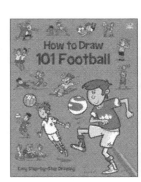
978-1-78244-536-4

978-1-84956-605-6

978-1-84956-607-0

978-1-84956-988-0

978-1-78244-486-2

978-1-78244-485-5

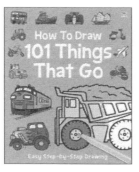
978-1-84956-616-2

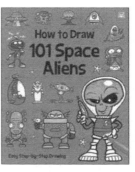
978-1-78244-483-1

978-1-84956-989-7

Practice Page

Practice Page

Printed in Great Britain
by Amazon